DAYS THAT SHOOK THE WORLD

THE RUSSIAN REVOLUTION

25 OCTOBER 1917

Paul Dowswell

an imprint of Hodder Children's Books

D1357129

DAYS THAT SHOOK THE WORLD

Assassination in Sarajevo
The Chernobyl Disaster
D-Day
The Dream of Martin Luther King Jr
The Fall of the Berlin Wall
The Freeing of Nelson Mandela
Hiroshima

The Invasion of Kuwait
The Kennedy Assassination
The Moon Landing
Pearl Harbor
The Russian Revolution
Tiananmen Square
The Wall Street Crash

Produced by Monkey Puzzle Media Ltd
Gissing's Farm, Fressingfield
Suffolk IP21 5SH, UK

First published in 2003 by Hodder Wayland
An imprint of Hodder Children's Books
Text copyright © 2003 Hodder Wayland
Volume copyright © 2003 Hodder Wayland

Series Concept: Liz Gogerly
Commissioning Editor: Jane Tyler
Editor: Patience Coster
Picture Researcher: Lynda Lines
Design: Jane Hawkins
Consultant: Michael Rawcliffe
Map artwork: Michael Posen

Cover picture: Bolsheviks pose for a photograph in Petrograd, October 1917.

Title page picture: This Communist propaganda painting from 1954 depicts Bolsheviks storming the Winter Palace in Petrograd in 1917.

We are grateful to the following for permission to reproduce photographs:
AKG 7 bottom, 22, 28 inset, 33; Art Archive 32 (Musée des Deux Guerres Mondiales, Paris/Dagli Orti); Associated Press 41 (Barry Thumma); Camera Press 14 (John Massey Stewart), 28, 39 bottom, 40 (Yevgenny Khaldei); Corbis 9 (Hulton-Deutsch Collection), 30, 35 (Bettmann); Novosti title page, 7 top, 11, 13, 21 bottom, 23, 24, 29, 31, 36, 37, 43 top, 46; Popperfoto 15, 16, 18, 19 bottom, 38 (ACQ), 42; Rex Features 43 bottom (Dmitry Beliakov); Topham Picturepoint front cover, 6, 8 bottom, 10, 12, 17, 19 top, 20, 21 top (Novosti), 25, 26 top, 27, 34, 39 top.

Printed in Hong Kong by Wing King Tong

British Library Cataloguing in Publication Data
Dowswell, Paul
  The Russian Revolution. - (Days that shook the world)
  1. Soviet Union - History - Revolution, 1917-1921 - Juvenile literature
  I.Title
  947'.0841

ISBN 0 7502 4411 9

Hodder Children's Books
A division of Hodder Headline Limited
338 Euston Road, London NW1 3BH

CONTENTS

THE SMOLNY INSTITUTE IN PETROGRAD, the capital city of Russia, seemed an unlikely venue for the Bolshevik Party's headquarters. It had been, after all, a school for prosperous, polite young ladies. But now, on 24 October 1917, it hummed and seethed with revolutionary activity – 'like a gigantic hive', said one American journalist. The girls had long gone, and the litter-strewn classrooms reeked of stale tobacco and urine. Here, under the steely direction of their leader, Vladimir Ilyich Lenin, the Bolsheviks were planning to seize Russia from the hands of the ailing Provisional Government. A Military Revolutionary Council (MRC) had been set up to oversee this.

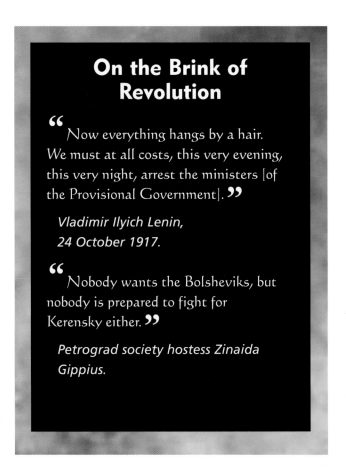

The Smolny Institute, St Petersburg, as it looks today. The former girls' private school was the Bolshevik headquarters during the October Revolution.

Outside, the atmosphere on the streets of the Russian capital was an odd mixture of chaos and normality. Theatres and restaurants were packed. At the opera the famous Fedor Chaliapin sang Verdi's *Don Carlos* to a full house. The city was bustling, but violent disorder was just a whisker away. Alexander Kerensky, the premier of the Provisional Government, was so overcome with the pressures of his job that he passed his days in a haze of morphine and brandy. His minister, Nikolai Sukhanov, recalled the feeling that power was 'hanging in the air'. Lenin, in disguise and hiding from the secret police at a secret address in the Vyborg district of Petrograd, decided that now was the moment to act.

The MRC had fixed a date for their uprising as 25 October, when the All-Russian Congress of Soviets (people's representatives) was to meet in Petrograd. Lenin wanted to seize power for the Bolsheviks, and

On the Brink of Revolution

" Now everything hangs by a hair. We must at all costs, this very evening, this very night, arrest the ministers [of the Provisional Government]. "

Vladimir Ilyich Lenin, 24 October 1917.

" Nobody wants the Bolsheviks, but nobody is prepared to fight for Kerensky either. "

Petrograd society hostess Zinaida Gippius.

present this to the Congress as a *fait accompli*. But, as fate would have it, the government brought about its own downfall. On the morning of 24 October, knowing that the Bolsheviks were planning to seize power, it moved against them. The MRC was outlawed, Bolshevik newspapers were closed down, and the police were given orders to arrest leaders of the party.

Lenin threw caution to the wind. That evening he travelled over to the Smolny Institute, hoping that a wig and a bandage over his face would prevent the police from recognizing him. His luck held. Arriving around midnight, he went at once to see Leon Trotsky – the most prominent member of the MRC. Trotsky was well prepared. He told Lenin that he had already issued orders for Bolshevik troops to seize key areas of the city. The Russian Revolution had begun.

Lenin photographed shortly before the Revolution. He has shaved his trademark beard and wears a wig to avoid being identified by the Russian police.

Soldiers loyal to the Bolsheviks stand guard outside the Smolny Institute during the autumn of 1917.

This photograph,
taken in around 1900,
gives some idea of the
squalor in which Russia's
peasants lived.

The State of the Nation

" The outside world should not be
surprised that we have an imperfect
government, but that we have any
government at all. With many
nationalities, many languages and a
nation largely illiterate [unable to read
or write], the marvel is that the country
can be held together even by
autocratic means. "

*Count Sergei Witte, Nicholas II's
minister of finance (1892-1903).*

AT THE START OF THE TWENTIETH
century Russia embraced a huge, sprawling
empire of many different languages and
cultures. Two thirds of the population were Slavs, but
the rest was made up of an assortment of 100
different nationalities. In the west, Russia bordered the
rival German and Austro-Hungarian empires. Her
southern borders stretched from the Caucasus
Mountains, past Afghanistan and on to Manchuria

and Japan. The far eastern tip of Siberia looked across
the Bering Straits to the United States' territory of
Alaska. These 22 million square kilometres and 130
million people would have been difficult enough for
a modern, well-organized government to control
effectively. Russia, however, was neither of these

things. The country was an old-fashioned autocracy; that is, a country ruled by a monarch who had absolute power. Unlike the leader of a democracy, the Russian monarch, who was called a Tsar, was not elected by the people; instead the throne was passed from generation to generation of the same family.

Although the country was beginning to develop the modern cities, industries and railways that were now well established in other more prosperous nations of Europe and North America, over 80 per cent of Russians were peasants. Most lived in small villages in conditions of extreme poverty, producing barely enough food for the ever-growing population to survive. In the new industrial towns and cities there were around three million inhabitants. Aside from the nobility and well-to-do middle class (known as the 'bourgeoisie'), most urban Russians lived and worked in circumstances of great hardship.

At the turn of the century, the Russian Tsar was Nicholas II. His coronation in 1896 had been blighted when more than a thousand people were trampled to death at a gathering in Moscow (see box). Nicholas was convinced this was a bad omen for his reign, and history would prove him right.

A Moment in Time

On a bright spring morning in May 1896, a huge crowd of half a million people gathers to celebrate the Tsar's coronation at a military training ground in the Moscow district of Khodynka. To mark the occasion, gifts, biscuits, free beer and sausages are issued. But as the crowd continues to grow a rumour spreads that there will not be enough for everyone. In the rush to grab whatever is going, 1,400 people are crushed to death and another 600 are injured. Despite the tragedy, the Russian Tsar, Nicholas II, is persuaded to continue with his celebrations. He attends a ball at the French Embassy that very evening. His insensitive behaviour in the wake of such a tragedy causes outrage among Moscow citizens.

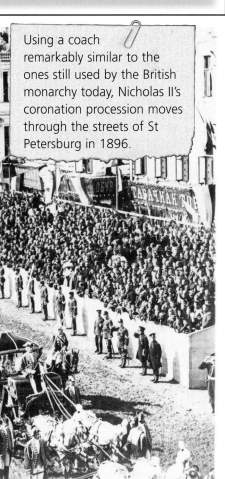

Using a coach remarkably similar to the ones still used by the British monarchy today, Nicholas II's coronation procession moves through the streets of St Petersburg in 1896.

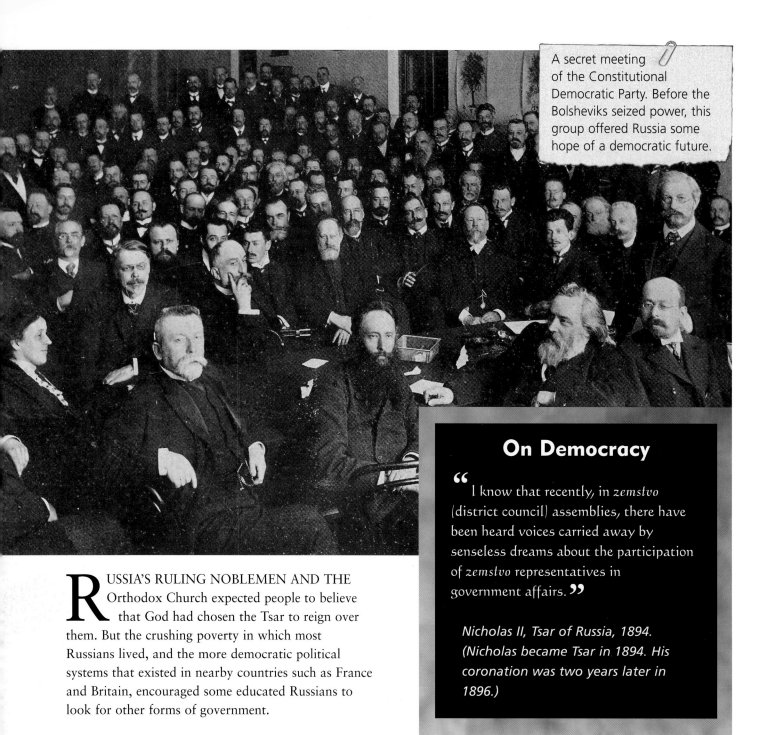

A secret meeting of the Constitutional Democratic Party. Before the Bolsheviks seized power, this group offered Russia some hope of a democratic future.

On Democracy

" I know that recently, in *zemstvo* (district council) assemblies, there have been heard voices carried away by senseless dreams about the participation of *zemstvo* representatives in government affairs. "

Nicholas II, Tsar of Russia, 1894. (Nicholas became Tsar in 1894. His coronation was two years later in 1896.)

RUSSIA'S RULING NOBLEMEN AND THE Orthodox Church expected people to believe that God had chosen the Tsar to reign over them. But the crushing poverty in which most Russians lived, and the more democratic political systems that existed in nearby countries such as France and Britain, encouraged some educated Russians to look for other forms of government.

The mildest of Nicholas' opponents were liberals, such as the Kadet Party (the Constitutional Democratic Party), which believed in Western democratic ideas. These liberals wanted Russia to become a constitutional monarchy similar to that of Britain, where the king shared power with a government elected by the people.

Further to the political left was the Social Democratic Labour Party. They believed that the workers and peasants should overthrow the Tsar and establish a communist state (see box opposite). The Social Democrats became a powerful political party after 1905, but before that they squabbled among themselves. In 1903 they split into two rival groups – Mensheviks and Bolsheviks. The Mensheviks believed that a revolution (an overthrow of the established order) would come about when Russia's workers were converted to the Menshevik cause. The Bolsheviks thought a revolution should be carried out by a party of professional revolutionaries, who would then impose a new political system on everyone else.

Finally there were the Social Revolutionaries. Their support was strongest among the peasants, whom they believed should take over farmland from Russia's landowners. Before the Revolution of 1905 (see page 12), they were the most violent opponents of the Tsar and were responsible for the assassinations of several leading government ministers.

Although opposition to the Tsar was illegal, education and public health reforms were put forward by local assemblies (gatherings) such as the *zemstvo*. But any opponent of the Tsar was likely to be investigated by a secret police organization called the Okhrana. Russians bold enough to oppose the Tsar's regime ran the risk of being murdered, imprisoned or exiled to faraway Siberia.

Other, more unofficial, opponents of change included, first and foremost, the ultra right-wing Union of the Russian People. Encouraged by the authorities, who often funded their activities, supporters of such organizations would beat up or murder liberal or left-wing opponents. Such groups were also violently anti-Jewish. An organization called the Black Hundred carried out pogroms against the Jews in support of the Tsar, who was an anti-Semite. So Russians opposed to the Tsar's regime were held back both by their own divisions and by fearsome opponents.

Marxism

Many of Russia's radical parties were inspired by the writings of the German philosopher, Karl Marx. Here, in brief, are the main ideas of Marxism:

- the workers should seize power from the landowners and factory bosses (the capitalists);

- when the capitalists have been overthrown and the workers hold power, a communist state should be created in which everyone will have an equal share in the wealth of their country, and the different social classes will disappear.

A society ball in St Petersburg, 1914, and a last glimpse of the glamour of the Russian court before war and revolution swept the old order away.

THE SERIES OF DEMONSTRATIONS AND disturbances that became known as the 1905 Revolution was provoked by Russia's involvement in a disastrous war with Japan over territory in Manchuria. In February 1904, intending to gain control of Manchuria, Japan attacked the Russian naval base of Port Arthur there. The Russian fleet set out from the Baltic Sea to defend its country's possession, which fell to the Japanese at the beginning of January 1905. After a seven-month journey, the fleet was destroyed by the Japanese navy at the Battle of Tsushima. (Only three out of twenty-seven Russian warships survived.) Russia was humiliated in the eyes of the world.

The fall of Port Arthur sparked off widespread murder, riots and rebellion in Russia, which had already been brewing following a series of bad harvests and rising unemployment. Most infamous among these disturbances was the 'Bloody Sunday' massacre in St Petersburg on 9 January 1905, where peaceful demonstrators were killed by troops (see box opposite). There was a wave of assassinations, including that of the Tsar's uncle, Grand Duke Sergei, the governor-general of Moscow. In towns, government officials were murdered, and in the countryside peasants rose up against their landlords and burned their houses. In June, the crew of the battleship *Potemkin* mutinied. This event particularly alarmed the Tsar, as he had never before doubted the loyalty of his armed forces. The unrest also provoked revolt among non-Russian people of the Empire, such as Armenians and Poles, who wanted their independence.

This illustration shows the Japanese capture of Port Arthur, the Russian navy base in Manchuria.

Most significant of all, Russia's workers and students began openly to form themselves into unions to protect their rights. This trend was particularly strong in St Petersburg, where a general strike in the autumn of 1905 caused the city to grind to a halt. Factories, schools and shops closed, and public transport ceased to operate. Strikers formed a grand council, called a Soviet, of 500 delegates representing 250,000 workers. This effective alternative to the existing local government organized its own defensive troops, arranged transport and food for its members, negotiated with employers, and even published its own newspaper. The idea of the Soviet was taken up in Moscow and in other towns throughout Russia.

A Moment in Time

On Sunday 9 January 1905, soon after first light, a crowd led by the priest Father Georgi Gapon gathers to march to the Winter Palace in St Petersburg. Its members hope to present a petition to the Tsar calling for political rights and an end to the war with Japan. Some 200,000 men, women and children, many dressed in their Sunday best and carrying portraits of the Tsar, walk through the snowy streets. As they near the Winter Palace, they are fired upon by ranks of soldiers. Among the 1,240 casualties, at least 370 are killed in an event that will come to be remembered as the 'Bloody Sunday' massacre. Father Gapon, who believed that the Tsar would receive them and listen to their pleas, is horrified. He stares at the carnage around him, crying over and over: 'There is no God any longer. There is no Tsar.'

Crowds flee in panic as soldiers in St Petersburg open fire on 9 January 1905. The event considerably undermined the Tsar in the eyes of many ordinary Russians.

A painting from the early 1900s shows the pomp and ceremony of Nicholas' rule. Here, seated third from the right at the long table in the background, he examines government documents.

THE RULE OF NICHOLAS II, THE FINAL TSAR OF the Romanov dynasty, was a perfect example of the weakness of autocracy as a political system. Even the shrewdest, most able politician on earth would have struggled with the immense problems faced by this feeble and dull man. Even he realized that he was not up to the job. The everyday workings of government bored him. When ministers tried to explain particular aspects of government policy he would stare blankly out of the window and pick his nose. It is difficult to imagine how Nicholas could believe in his God-given right to rule and at the same time display a complete lack of interest in politics. But even his own father had once described him to a minister as 'a dunce'. However, for all his faults, at least Nicholas was a dutiful Tsar. He was so intent on the small details of ruling that he even stamped his own letters and personally approved minor requests, such as changes in surname.

Unfit to Rule

" What is going to happen to me and to all of Russia? I am not prepared to be a Tsar. I never wanted to become one. I know nothing of the business of ruling. I have no idea of even how to talk to the ministers. "

Nicholas II, on becoming Tsar in 1894.

" He only understands the significance of some isolated fact, without connection with the rest.... He sticks to his insignificant, petty point of view. "

Konstantin Pobedonostsev, his tutor.

Both quoted in The People's Tragedy *by Orlando Figes, an epic account of the Russian Revolution.*

In matters of learning Nicholas was not entirely without talent. He was a gifted linguist. Along with his native Russian, he spoke French, German and perfect English. He and his wife Alexandra always used English when speaking to one another, and in manners, appearance and upbringing they both could easily have passed as English. (They even called each other 'Hubby' and 'Wifey'.)

Alexandra was a German princess whom Nicholas had married against the wishes of his father. She had been brought up in the court of Britain's Queen Victoria and spoke Russian very badly. More than anyone, she encouraged her husband to play the autocrat. A distant and arrogant figure, she was disliked both by her fellow courtiers and the Russian people. Disastrously for the Tsar, she took an active interest in politics.

History dealt both Nicholas and Alexandra a cruel hand. But for them personally, at least until the Revolution of 1917, their greatest tragedy was their son Alexis' haemophilia. In this awful, crippling condition, even the slightest cut or bruise can lead to fatal internal bleeding. Their search for a cure for their son's illness led them into the hands of Rasputin, who has come to be seen as one of history's most infamous villains, and further undermined their standing in the eyes of the ordinary Russian people.

The doomed dynasty – Nicholas, Alexandra, their four daughters and the haemophiliac heir to the throne, Alexis.

GRIGORI RASPUTIN ARRIVED IN ST PETERSBURG in 1903. Although he came from peasant stock, he claimed to have trained as a monk and said he possessed magical powers. Gossip about Rasputin reached the Romanov court and, by 1905, he had become a favourite of the royal family. Alexandra was particularly drawn to him because he seemed able to ease the suffering of her haemophiliac son. Either by coincidence, or by some phenomenon still unknown to medical science, Rasputin's presence, touch or prayers seemed to produce a rapid improvement in the boy, especially when he was suffering from potentially fatal tumours or fever brought on by his condition.

Photographs of Rasputin clearly show his extraordinary, hypnotic gaze, stocky build and filthy appearance. What is missing from such visual records is his awful smell – said to have resembled that of a goat. Curiously, Rasputin soon developed a reputation as a womaniser, and he seduced many of St Petersburg's wealthiest women. It was widely believed that he was Alexandra's lover too, but there is no evidence to suggest this was the case.

Nicholas was not as smitten by Rasputin as his wife was, but he appreciated the calming effect the monk had on her. 'Better one Rasputin than ten fits of hysterics every day', he once remarked, rather unkindly. Yet he too found Rasputin to be a source of comfort and reassurance.

Rasputin's downfall was his lust for power. He showed no great interest in wealth, but he loved to be in a position of influence. Civil servants, government ministers, even officials of the Church, all had to win the favour of Rasputin to advance their careers.

Grigori Rasputin, surrounded by the aristocratic ladies of St Petersburg, fixes the camera with his baleful gaze.

More than any other of Nicholas and Alexandra's failings, it was Rasputin's close relationship with them that did the most to undermine the respect ordinary people had for their Tsar and his wife. When the First World War broke out in 1914, Rasputin was even allowed to interfere in the running of the Russian army campaigns. Such was his influence with the royal family that he was able to have good government ministers and army generals replaced by incompetent ones who were loyal to him. He was bringing such shame and disrepute to the Tsar that eventually a group of noblemen banded together to kill him.

After the Russian Revolution, Rasputin was depicted in Bolshevik propaganda as the embodiment of evil. But in many respects he was no more evil and corrupt than the aristocratic courtiers who were envious of his influence over the Romanovs and of the power and charisma possessed by this simple peasant.

A Moment in Time

On the evening of 29 December 1916, Rasputin is lured to the home of the beautiful Grand Duchess Irana. As he waits to see the duchess, he is given poisoned wine and cakes laced with cyanide. These apparently have no effect on him whatsoever, so Prince Felix Yusulov shoots him three times with a pistol. Then his body is weighed down with iron chains and thrown into the River Neva. When Rasputin's body is washed up two days later, it is noted that before he died he managed to undo many of his chains and that his lungs are full of water. Despite the poison and the bullets, he had actually died from drowning.

The royal family's relationship with Rasputin was a gift to their enemies. Here a cartoon depicts Nicholas and Alexandra as docile puppets, dominated by Rasputin's evil influence.

FOLLOWING THE UPHEAVAL OF 1905, THE TSAR was persuaded by his prime minister, Sergei Witte, to make political changes to prevent further violence. In October 1905, Russians were provided with a series of reforms known as the October Manifesto (see box below). These provided a constitution and divided the revolutionaries. As striking workers drifted back to their jobs in the factories, troops broke up the St Petersburg and Moscow Soviets, and prominent revolutionaries fled or were arrested and exiled.

In May 1906 Witte was dismissed and Nicholas issued another set of rulings (the Fundamental Laws), which gave him total control over the Duma (Parliament), allowing him to dismiss it if it criticized him. This he did on two occasions, in 1906 and 1907. Then new laws changed the system of voting, enabling the richest people in Russia, who were the Tsar's greatest supporters, to elect two-thirds of the representatives to the Duma. This produced a Duma that supported the Tsar uncritically.

In June 1906 Peter Stolypin became prime minister. Stolypin clearly understood that the government needed to improve the lives of ordinary people if it were to rescue the Russian monarchy from disaster. He steered a clever path between reform and repression. The more able peasants were encouraged to break away from their communes and become independent farmers. But more than a thousand peasants were executed for their part in rural riots. Some of the Tsar's ministers were hostile to Stolypin and he was assassinated in 1911, with his reforms only half completed.

The October Manifesto

- All Russian men have the right to vote.

- An elected parliament called the Duma is to be set up.

- Any new Russian law has to be approved by the Duma.

- Russians are allowed to form political parties.

- Free speech shall be permitted, along with the right to hold meetings.

Peter Stolypin, arguably the Tsar's most able prime minister, had enemies both inside and outside the government.

In 1912 this group of Russian mineworkers was shot dead by troops because they had gone on strike.

Following the Revolution of 1905 there was a lull, but unrest soon returned to the cities, especially St Petersburg and Moscow. In 1914, in the month before the start of the First World War, St Petersburg was paralyzed by strikes. Workers and police fought hand-to-hand battles on the streets. Most ominous of all for the government was the sea of red flags brandished by the strikers. The red flag was the symbol of the left-wing socialist parties. The continued unrest was all the more disappointing for the government, as advances in Russian industry were beginning to produce the beginnings of prosperity for some of its people.

The outbreak of the First World War could have tipped the striking workers of Russia into outright revolution. But the opposite happened. When war with Germany and Austro-Hungary began on 1 August 1914, the Bolsheviks condemned Russia's involvement in the conflict. But throughout Russia, peasants and workers rallied to support Nicholas II and their country. The war, it seemed, had forged a fresh bond between the Tsar and his people.

Nicholas II blesses his troops as they prepare to leave for the front line at the start of the First World War.

Weary soldiers trudge through the streets of a Russian city. The Tsar's unsuccessful command of his armies lost him further support among the Russian people.

ORDINARY RUSSIANS MAY HAVE FLOCKED TO defend their homeland when war broke out, but the course of the war made the Russian Revolution almost inevitable. For the Tsar's regime, one disaster followed another: Nicholas's conduct following the Khodynka tragedy (see page 9), his inflexibility and that of his despised German wife, the 'Bloody Sunday' massacre at the Winter Palace in 1905 (see page 13), the scandal of Rasputin, and finally the horror of the First World War.

With equipment in short supply, some soldiers were sent into battle without boots or rifles (they were expected to pick up a gun from a fallen comrade). Generals squandered the lives of their men in assaults that turned into massacres. Before the war was a year old, Russia had suffered almost four million casualties and the German army had advanced 450 kilometres into Russian territory. Millions of civilians had become refugees, and the threat of famine loomed over the empire. Dismayed by the course of the war, Nicholas II left St Petersburg (now renamed Petrograd, because it sounded less German). The Tsar assumed command of the armed forces at the front, leaving the control of the country to Alexandra and, unofficially, to Rasputin.

Petrograd citizens queue for bread in 1917. The dreadful hardships of the war, both for soldiers and civilians, brought the Tsar's regime crashing down.

On 22 February 1917, the situation reached breaking point. Protests in Petrograd against poor living conditions turned into mass strikes and demonstrations, with workers calling for bread and peace. Over the next two days, crowds attacked public buildings and police stations, and lawlessness overtook large parts of the city. Troops called out to restore order refused to fire on the demonstrators. By 25 February, most of the 170,000 soldiers of the Petrograd garrison had joined the protesters. As in 1905, Soviets were set up in factories and within the army, in the capital and in other major cities. From February until October, the grandly named Petrograd Soviet of Workers' and Soldiers' Deputies remained strong in the city. Within these Soviets, support for the Bolshevik Party was growing stronger.

On 27 February, party leaders in the Duma formed an emergency committee to restore order. A new Provisional Government was formed, led by a prominent liberal, Prince George Lvov. By now, both government and military leaders had lost faith in Nicholas, and he was asked to abdicate. His spirit broken, Nicholas reluctantly agreed. No decision could be reached on who should succeed him, so on 3 March Nicholas's Romanov dynasty, and the thousand-year-old Russian monarchy, came to an end.

The Power of the Soviet

"The Provisional Government does not possess any real power; and its directives [orders] are carried out only to the extent that it is permitted by the Soviet... which enjoys all the elements of real power, since the troops, the railways, the post and telegraph are all in its hands. One can say flatly that the Provisional Government exists only so long as it is permitted by the Soviet. "

Provisional Government war minister Alexander Guchkov.

Crowds burn the Romanov royal crest during street protests in February 1917.

IN EARLY 1917 THE PETROGRAD SOVIET WAS LED BY a combination of Mensheviks and Social Revolutionaries. Even the rival Bolsheviks were united with them in support for the Provisional Government against the Tsar. Among the Bolshevik leaders, only Lenin was calling for an immediate Bolshevik seizure of power. But, as a political enemy of the Tsar, he had been in exile in Switzerland since 1907, and was still there.

Since the beginning of the First World War, the Bolsheviks had been receiving money from the German government, which funded their activities in the hope of undermining the Tsar's regime. In March 1917, the Germans seized their moment and provided a locked and guarded train to take Lenin back to Russia. He arrived at Petrograd's Finland Station on 3 April to a hero's welcome. Carried shoulder high by the crowd, he made a rousing speech urging them to remove the Provisional Government. That night, he laid out his strategy to his fellow Bolsheviks. The Soviets should seize control of the country and end the war. The banks, farms, factories and machinery of government should be placed under Bolshevik control. Lenin was plainly calling for a second, and far greater, revolution.

The speech met with little support among the Bolsheviks, and horrified their political rivals. But such was Lenin's skill as a leader and speaker that he soon had his party behind him. Bolshevik slogans such as 'Land, Peace and Bread' and 'All Power to the Soviets' captured the imagination of people increasingly disillusioned with the Provisional Government. The Bolsheviks were building a formidable body of support.

This dramatic photograph shows the moment troops opened fire on demonstrators in Petrograd during a Bolshevik-inspired uprising in July 1917.

Two days of Bolshevik-inspired rioting in July led to a government crackdown. The party headquarters were raided, and the Bolshevik newspaper, *Pravda* (Truth), was shut down. Lenin was denounced as a German spy, and fled to Finland. For now, the Provisional Government could still command control of the police and army, but their weak hold on power was slipping. Strikes and rural riots continued, and roaming bands of army deserters spread mayhem and terror.

This breakdown in law and order prompted a coup by General Lavr Kornilov, the commander-in-chief of the Russian forces. Believing he had the support of the Provisional Government, which had been led since July by socialist lawyer Alexander Kerensky, Kornilov ordered his troops to march on Petrograd with the intention of massacring the Soviet. But the coup collapsed into farce as Russian railway workers refused to transport the soldiers. Fear of a counter-revolution like this one increased support for the Bolsheviks, who won control of the Petrograd and Moscow Soviets. Lenin was sure his time had come.

Vladimir Ilych Lenin (1870-1924)

Born into a middle-class family, Lenin became a committed revolutionary following the execution of his elder brother in 1887 for plotting to kill the Tsar. Lenin trained as a lawyer and graduated with a first-class degree from St Petersburg University. He first came into contact with the Bolsheviks while working as a lawyer. Described by American journalist John Reed as 'a short, stocky figure, with a big head set down on his shoulders', Lenin bristled with determination and conviction.

'History will never forgive us if we do not seize power now,' he wrote from Finland. Assuming his disguise once more, Lenin returned to the streets of Petrograd.

As Russian society collapsed into chaos, troops on the front line deserted in droves. These men are trying to return to their home villages.

Midnight to 2.00 am All around Petrograd, troops and workers who supported the Bolsheviks began to seize the bridges, railway stations, telephone exchanges, power plants, banks and post offices of the city.

2.00 am As the city clocks struck the hour, their chimes drifted across a bright, bitterly cold, moonlit night. In an office at the Smolny Institute, Trotsky turned to Lenin and said: 'It's begun.' The fugitive Lenin was overawed by a sense of history being made. 'From being on the run to supreme power – that's too much,' he said to Trotsky. 'It makes me dizzy.'

7.00 am Kerensky was asleep in his quarters at the Winter Palace. He awoke to find the building partially surrounded by Bolshevik troops. Knowing he could not call on the city's own garrison, which supported the Soviet, he decided to leave Petrograd and get help from loyal troops on the Russian front line. He could not take the train as the railway workers supported the Soviet, so he decided to drive to the front. But the Bolsheviks had disabled all the government cars.

The Struggle of the Masses

" The situation is critical in the extreme. It is absolutely clear that to delay the insurrection now will be inevitably fatal. I exhort my comrades with all my heart and strength to realize that everything now hangs by a thread, that we are being confronted by problems that cannot be solved by conferences and congresses… but exclusively by the people, the masses, by the struggle of the armed masses. "

Lenin's analysis of Russia on the eve of 25 October.

In a Moscow street in 1917 a Bolshevik supporter hands out political leaflets to an eager crowd.

Armed Bolsheviks pose for a propaganda photograph on the streets of Petrograd in October 1917.

10.00 am By now, the Bolshevik forces had taken all their major objectives save one – the Winter Palace. This was guarded by a haphazard band of cadets and female troops, known as the Women's Shock Battalion of Death. Over at the Smolny Institute, Lenin was so confident of success that he put the finishing touches to his declaration announcing the overthrow of the Provisional Government, and the seizure of power by the Bolsheviks.

11.00 am Kerensky's aides finally located a car at the American embassy. Kerensky was driven out of the Winter Palace in a Renault, a French car, flying the 'Stars and Stripes', the American flag. Troops loyal to the Bolsheviks stepped back from the road as he passed by unrecognized. The car left Petrograd heading for the Russian front.

Myth and Reality

Ten years after the Revolution, the legendary Russian director Sergei Eisenstein made a film called *October*, which marked the events in Petrograd. One of the great masterpieces of black-and-white cinema, it shows the Revolution unfolding in a sequence of swirling mob scenes with high heroics and breathless drama. Although audiences in the Soviet Union were encouraged to believe this version as the truth, the images in the film were nothing like what happened in real life. In the West, clips from *October* have been used in history documentaries in place of genuine newsreel. They have added to the myth that 25 October was a day of great battles and daring bravery. It is interesting to note that more damage was done to the Winter Palace during the filming of *October* than in the Revolution of 1917.

Petrograd at the time of the Russian Revolution.

KEY:
1. Peter and Paul Fortress
2. Winter Palace
3. Marinsky Palace
4. Tauride Palace
5. Smolny Institute

1 mile
1 km

The Provisional Government during a meeting in Petrograd in 1917. Alexander Kerensky is sixth from the left, in the centre of the picture.

3.00 pm The Winter Palace was now surrounded by Bolshevik soldiers. It was so poorly defended that they could have stormed it with little resistance. But their commanders were cautious. It was thought that guns in the Fortress of St Peter and St Paul on the opposite bank of the River Neva could be used to bombard the Palace. But they were found to be rusty and unusable. New field guns were brought up, but there was no suitable ammunition for them. The bombardment would have to wait.

Lenin told the Petrograd Soviet that the Provisional Government had been overthrown. He was so desperate to inform the All-Russian Congress of Soviets of the Bolsheviks' seizure of power that he was not prepared to wait any longer for confirmation.

Inside the Winter Palace, troop morale was low. Soldiers sat around smoking and drinking. They became less and less prepared to lay down their lives to support the Provisional Government. Many openly discussed leaving the Palace. This was remarkably easy. The vast 1,500-room building had many entrances and exits, and most of these were unguarded.

Midday Bolshevik troops seized the Marinsky Palace, headquarters of the Preparliament – a government body set up after the February Revolution until a legitimate parliament could be elected in its place. Inside the Winter Palace, news of Kerensky's departure provoked widespread panic. Remaining ministers of the Provisional Government met in the Malachite Hall to discuss a last-ditch defence.

2.30 pm Lenin and Trotsky held an emergency session of the Petrograd Soviet, and declared that the Bolsheviks had seized power, and that a new Soviet government would be formed immediately.

6.00 pm Over at the Tauride Palace, the seat of the Duma, representatives decided they should march over to the Winter Palace to defend the Provisional Government. Three hundred elderly deputies, led by the white-bearded mayor of Petrograd, Grigori Schreider, marched out of the building carrying food for the defenders. They had not marched very far, however, before they were stopped by a group of Bolshevik sailors who could not believe that these old men were willing to sacrifice their lives. The Duma deputies turned back, their moment of bravery past.

6.50 pm The Bolsheviks issued an ultimatum to the Winter Palace, calling on the Provisional Government to surrender. It was presented to ministers who had just sat down to dine on *borscht* (beetroot soup), steamed fish and artichokes. Still unsure of when Kerensky would be returning with help, and unaware of their own laughable weakness, they decided to try to hold out.

7.00 pm Of the 3,000 troops who had been inside the Winter Palace that morning, all but 300 had now fled. As they had been left without rations, most simply left the Palace as discreetly as they could and headed for one of Petrograd's many restaurants.

Reasons for Revolution

" *What everybody needed were not empires, but bread, salt and candles.* "

The novelist Boris Pasternak on what he believed to be the cause of the Russian Revolution.

Russian soldiers, declaring their allegiance with the Bolshevik red flag that flies above them, mass outside the Tauride Palace during the Revolution.

9.40 pm The *Aurora*, a Bolshevik-controlled gunship anchored near to the Winter Palace on the River Neva, fired a single, blank round. The sound reverberated throughout the city, and caused panic inside the Palace. Everyone dropped to the floor.

10.40 pm The Soviet Congress opened at the Smolny Institute. There were 650 representatives present, from the Bolshevik, Menshevik and Social Revolutionary parties. The Bolsheviks were the largest party, but they did not have an outright majority. Amid the thick tobacco smoke in the meeting hall, there was an atmosphere of wild excitement.

11.00 pm Bolshevik forces at the St Peter and St Paul Fortress across the River Neva from the Winter Palace began to fire shells at it. Almost all fell short and into the river.

Midnight As guns thundered outside the Soviet Congress, the Mensheviks and Social Revolutionaries demanded that fighting stop at once. Such action, they rightly predicted, would topple Russia into civil war. The Bolsheviks refused to listen to them. Their opponents walked out, as Trotsky delivered one of the most famous dismissals in history (see first quote opposite). Lenin had cleverly undermined his opponents, leaving the Bolsheviks in complete control of the Soviet.

The *Aurora* gunship at anchor on the River Neva. A blank fired from one of her guns heralded the final collapse of opposition to the Bolsheviks within the Winter Palace.

Tsarist troops inside the Winter Palace, shortly before it was stormed by the Bolsheviks.

Communist propaganda, including cinema and official art, painted the Revolution as a day of great drama – which it transparently wasn't.

(2.00 am) The Russian justice minister, Malyantovich, ordered his soldiers not to resist the Bolshevik troops trying to occupy the Palace. A Bolshevik officer, Vladimir Antonov-Ovseenko, entered the ministerial offices and announced: 'In the name of the Military and Revolutionary Committee of the Petrograd Soviet, I declare the Provisional Government deposed!' Members of the government present in the Palace were immediately arrested. They were marched over to be imprisoned in the St Peter and St Paul Fortress by a platoon of Bolshevik soldiers. Several times the soldiers had to prevent members of a crowd of onlookers from lynching the men. When news of the fall of the Palace reached the Smolny Institute, the Bolsheviks immediately proclaimed that the Soviets were now in power throughout Russia.

The number of casualties on the day was amazingly low – six Bolshevik soldiers had been killed (two of them unlucky enough to be shot accidentally by their own comrades). There were no Provisional Government fatalities. But shortly after the fall of the Winter Palace Bolshevik soldiers discovered its vast wine cellar. The next morning a drunken orgy of indiscriminate vandalism and killing would be visited upon an unfortunate selection of Petrograd's wealthier citizens.

Revolutionary Talk

“ You are miserable bankrupts, your role is played out; go where you ought to go – into the dustbin of history. ”
Leon Trotsky's words to his departing opponents in the Soviet Congress.

“ We completely untied the Bolsheviks' hands, making them masters of the whole situation and yielding to them the whole arena of the Revolution… by leaving the Congress, we ourselves gave the Bolsheviks a monopoly of the Soviet, of the masses, and of the Revolution. ”
Menshevik leader Nikolai Sukhanov looking back on the Revolution from 1921.

“ This final act of revolution seems, after all this, too brief, too dry, too businesslike – somehow out of correspondence with the historic scope of events. ”
Leon Trotsky, 1917.

Russia's new masters, the Bolshevik Red Guard, stand in front of the Petrograd State Bank shortly after the events of 25 October 1917.

On the evening of 26 October, Lenin made a triumphant address to the All-Russian Congress of Soviets in the ballroom of the Smolny Institute. His daring had won the day. Standing before the cheering crowd, he began his speech with the ringing phrase: 'We shall now proceed to construct the socialist order.'

Now that they were in power, Lenin's Bolsheviks set about transforming Russian society. Factories, banks and land were claimed by the state. Law courts and town councils were replaced with 'People's Tribunals' and local Soviets. The Church, a central pillar of the Tsarist regime, was allowed to continue its routines and customs, but its lands were confiscated and religious teaching was banned in schools. Men and women were declared equal, and centuries-old Tsarist laws unfavourable to women concerning marriage and divorce were abolished.

However, power in Petrograd did not, of course, mean power throughout the huge sprawling Russian Empire. Immediately following the events in Petrograd, the Soviet in Moscow had to fight for ten days to establish its authority against military cadets and students who remained loyal to the Provisional Government. Such divisions and conflicts were a foretaste of the civil war that was to come in Russia. Lured by promises of immediate peace, most towns and cities welcomed the Bolshevik regime. But the Bolsheviks' old rivals, the Social Revolutionaries, still had the greatest support in the countryside.

The Bolsheviks had no intention that theirs would be a democratic regime. They had seized power in the name of the Soviets, but all along had intended to concentrate that power in their own hands. In November 1917, elections for the Constituent Assembly (Russia's first democratically elected national legislature – a group of people with the power to make or change laws) produced a Social Revolutionary majority. In January 1918, the Assembly held its first meeting and immediately rejected a motion to back Lenin's government. At once, Bolshevik soldiers broke the meeting up. From that moment on, the Bolsheviks were completely open about their plans for a dictatorship. A new secret police service called the Cheka replaced the Okhrana. The Cheka set itself the task of arresting 'counter-revolutionaries' – virtually anyone opposed to the Bolsheviks. Although the people in charge of Russia had changed, their methods of ensuring obedience to their regime remained very much the same, or worse.

A Worker Writes...

" ...it is unpleasant and humiliating to recall (the) gentry, but it is even more unpleasant and humiliating to meet the same kind of 'old masters' at the present time. I know very many comrades who occupy various responsible posts in unions and committees, and when you happen to turn to them with some enquiry... they answer either rudely and arrogantly, or they do not answer at all. "

This letter, from an anonymous 'working man', appeared in the Petrograd newspaper, Krasnaya Gazeta (Red Gazette), a year after the October Revolution. The author complains that the Bolsheviks are behaving like the 'old masters' – Russia's landowners and aristocrats before the Revolution.

The Bolsheviks made concerted efforts to humiliate their 'class enemies' – Russia's 'bourgeoisie' – seen here clearing snow from a city street in 1918.

A Soviet poster appealing to foreign workers to join Russians in overthrowing their oppressors. But the expected revolutionary upheaval throughout Europe did not occur.

WHILE RUSSIA WAS IMMERSED IN its Revolution, the German army swept into Russian territory in the Baltic and Poland. At first, the Bolsheviks were not greatly concerned by this loss of land. They hoped, as Karl Marx had predicted, that other countries would soon follow their example. If this were to happen, the capitalist democracies and dynasties of Europe would be swept away in a frenzy of further workers' revolutions. But this did not happen, although Germany hovered on the brink of a communist revolution of its own when it lost the First World War one year later.

As commissar for foreign affairs, Leon Trotsky was responsible for making peace with Germany and Austro-Hungary. He was in a pitifully weak position. The Russian army was now a shadow of its already ineffective self. The Revolution had accelerated the mass desertions suffered by the military, and what troops remained at the front were ill-equipped and underfed. A new German offensive in February 1918 smashed through the Russian front lines and saw German troops head deep into the Ukraine. Many members of Russia's middle and upper classes were hoping that German troops would soon reach Petrograd and Moscow, and free them from the strange new regime that had seized their wealth and power.

Lenin and Trotsky were well aware of this threat to their Revolution. They were forced to negotiate a 'peace at any price' settlement with the Central Powers (Germany, Austro-Hungary and Turkey). Agreement was reached at the Polish town of Brest-Litovsk on 3 March 1918. The terms were a catastrophic humiliation for Russia. The industrial areas around the Baltic (Finland, Estonia, Latvia, Lithuania and Poland) and the rich agricultural land of the Ukraine were handed over. The Ukraine was returned to Russia, after the defeat of the Central Powers in the First World War in November 1918, but the rest of the territory lost at Brest-Litovsk remained so.

The Bolsheviks still hoped that their enemies would soon be preoccupied with socialist revolutions of their own. But while the immediate prospect of a takeover by Germany and Austro-Hungary was avoided, inside Russia there loomed an even greater threat to the Bolshevik regime.

Land Lost at Brest-Litovsk

Russia handed over territory consisting of:

- one-third of its agricultural land
- four-fifths of its coal mines
- a quarter of its railways
- one-third of its factories
- a quarter of its population
- The Central Powers also demanded that Russia pay reparations totalling 6,000 million marks.

Bolshevik delegates are forced to negotiate a humiliating peace with the Central Powers at Brest-Litovsk in March 1918.

Zensiert
Paul Hoffmann & Co.
Berlin-Schöneberg.

X

phot. Bild-und Film-Am
1775.

Der Waffenstillstand von Brest-Litowsk.
Prinz Leopold von Bayern (X) beim Unterzeichnen des Waffenstillstandes.

This graphic Bolshevik propaganda poster shows a Russian worker bombarding a bourgeois 'White' general with the fruits of his hard, manual labour.

WITH HINDSIGHT, THE OUTBREAK OF CIVIL WAR in Russia was inevitable. A small group of determined revolutionaries had seized power in the Russian capital and were attempting to impose their politics on a huge country. It was obvious they would face powerful opposition.

During early 1918, forces hostile to the Bolsheviks began to gather. Chief among them were many of the Tsar's former officers, who were strongly supported by Russia's former allies, France and Britain. Not only did the Allies want to bring Russia back into the war against Germany, they felt intensely hostile towards the Marxist politics of the new regime. (British

minister of munitions Winston Churchill, for example, spoke of the 'plague' of Bolshevism.)

The enemies of the Bolshevik Revolution called themselves 'Whites', and presented a formidable threat. By the summer of 1918 they controlled great swathes of eastern Russia and were advancing rapidly towards Moscow.

Once again, Leon Trotsky showed what a remarkable asset he was to the Bolsheviks. Now appointed commissar for war, he organized a concerted communist opposition to the Whites in the shape of the 'Red' Army. The Bolshevik Red Army had few supporters among the officer class, so the quality of its leadership was poor. But with determined ruthlessness, Trotsky conscripted former Tsarist officers, blackmailing them into fighting for the Bolsheviks by threatening to murder their families. The loyalty of the rank-and-file soldiers was also secured by the appointment of military commissars who ensured that desertion was punished by execution.

Trotsky directed the efforts of the Red Army with extraordinary vigour. Surrounded on at least three sides, he sped from front to front in a special armoured train, encouraging and terrifying his forces with his passionate speeches and dire threats.

The war was fought with horrendous savagery on both sides. Prisoners and hostages were massacred. Each side fiercely guarded its territory, and anyone found who was suspected of supporting the other side faced instant execution. For the Bolsheviks, the war took a turn for the worse in November 1918, when Germany surrendered to the Allies. Now the Allies could concentrate on their former ally, Russia. French and British soldiers from the trenches of the western front were despatched to fight for the Whites, but this was never a popular cause. Troops who had just

suffered four years of war had little inclination to fight for a cause with which they had no real connection. Under Trotsky's unflinching leadership, the Red Army drove off its attackers, and by the end of 1920 the civil war had ended in a Bolshevik victory.

The End of the Royal Family

After his abdication, Nicholas II and his family had been shuffled around from one secure spot to another while both the Provisional Government and the Bolsheviks decided what to do with them. By the summer of 1918 the royal family was held in a house in the Urals town of Ekaterinburg. When White forces threatened to occupy the territory, the local Soviet, terrified that Nicholas would be rescued, decided on drastic action. The royal family were taken to the cellar and brutally murdered with guns and bayonets. The bodies were then burned with petrol, dissolved in sulphuric acid, and dumped in a mine shaft.

White Russian troops, somewhere in Siberia during the civil war, advance on horseback.

Grain seized by the Bolsheviks, as part of their 'war communism' policy, is stored inside a church.

B Y 1921 THE FIRST WORLD WAR, THE Revolution, the treaty with the Central Powers, and civil war had left Russia ravaged and drained. Its factories and railways were in ruins, and its farmland lay desolate. Over the next two years some five million people would die from starvation and disease.

Unsurprisingly, the economy was near to collapse, and inflation had made the value of money almost worthless. Russians resorted to primitive barter, and even the government was reduced to paying wages in food and goods – a measure known as 'war communism'. Some Bolsheviks welcomed this collapse of the monetary system, reasoning that money should not be needed in a communist society and that barter was preferable. But most Russians suffered terribly

during this time of economic chaos. One of the most unpopular government measures was the forced seizure of grain from peasants to provide for the revolutionaries' main supporters, the urban workers. Just as social breakdown had led directly to the Revolution of 1917, so it produced further open rebellion against the Bolsheviks.

Lenin recognized that drastic action had to be taken to stop this new threat to his emerging communist state. In March 1921 the Bolsheviks introduced the New Economic Policy (NEP), a series of measures designed to win back support for the regime. Trading and small-scale industries were returned to private ownership. Bigger industrial concerns, still owned by the state, were encouraged to take account of profits and losses in an attempt to make them more efficient.

In the countryside, instead of seizing grain the government took some of it as a tax, which made the process seem more official and fairer. Peasants were then allowed to sell what they had left for profit.

The NEP was a tremendous success. As a result, agricultural and industrial production increased rapidly. This allowed the government to begin to concentrate on measures that would improve the lives of ordinary Russian people. Although rationing, low wages and unemployment were still widespread, resources were now available to assist with the improvement of housing, health care and education. In a country well known for its backwardness, Lenin was keen to establish the idea that his Bolsheviks were the party of progress. But beside these positive changes,

the Bolsheviks were becoming increasingly intolerant of any criticism of their regime. In March 1921, Lenin declared a ban on all opposition groups within the party. The Cheka, the Bolshevik secret police first introduced in the weeks after the Revolution, became known as the OGPU. With its huge network of spies and informers, the OGPU kept a stiflingly close watch on the activities and opinions of ordinary citizens.

As the Bolsheviks grew more confident in their hold on power, they turned on the Church. Karl Marx had famously dismissed religion as 'the opium of the people' – meaning that the Church was a distraction from the realities of life – and all right-thinking Bolsheviks were atheists. In the early 1920s many of Russia's ornate and beautiful churches were damaged or destroyed. Priests were beaten up and 6,000 of them were murdered.

Secure in their power, the Bolsheviks turned on the Church, which they saw as a decadent ally of the former regime.

Communism Defined

Lenin's vision for the future of his country was of a modern industrial nation controlled by communist Soviets. In 1920 he summed this up in the following slogan:

"Communism is Soviet power, plus the electrification of the whole country."

A whiff of Stalin's character can be gleaned from his steely gaze, as he converses with Lenin in around 1920.

A Rude Man

" Stalin is too rude. This fault is intolerable in a Secretary. I propose to comrades that they find a way of removing Stalin and appointing another man who is more patient, more loyal, more polite and is considerate to his comrades. "

Vladimir Ilyich Lenin, 1923. Extract from Lenin's secret Political Testament.

During the great upheaval of the first year of the Bolshevik regime, Lenin was wounded in an assassination attempt. His health never really recovered, and the strain of leading the first communist country aged him quickly. In May 1922, at the age of 52, he suffered the first of several strokes. His mind and body gradually deteriorated, although he remained nominal head of his country until his death on 21 January 1924.

As Lenin faded, so other Bolsheviks began to gain greater control over communist policy. Alongside Leon Trotsky, potential future leaders included Grigori Zinoviev, Leon Kamenev and Josef Stalin. Under their direction, Russia became a more centralized state – meaning that an increasing number of decisions were taken by the government in the capital, which had been moved from Petrograd to Moscow in 1918. In 1922, the country was renamed the Union of Soviet Socialist Republics (USSR), also known as the Soviet Union. Outlying regions of the former Russian Empire, such as Azerbaijan and Turkestan, which were culturally different from Russia, were forced to join this union.

The charismatic and capable Trotsky seemed an obvious successor to Lenin, although his boundless confidence irritated some of his comrades. Stalin was everything Trotsky was not. Small and physically unremarkable, he seemed such a dull and plodding character that his critics nicknamed him 'Comrade Card-Index' because he had details of all the party members on file. Stalin was a great organizer and had immense cunning. His position as the general secretary of the Communist Party allowed him to appoint his supporters to key positions of power. In this way he amassed a great deal of influence. After Lenin's death,

Stalin set about expelling his rivals for power from the party. In 1929 he banished Trotsky from the Soviet Union. Trotsky ended up in Mexico, where he was assassinated in 1940, almost certainly on Stalin's orders.

As leader of the Soviet Union, Stalin became one of the most feared dictators of the twentieth century. Under his rule, ordinary Russians endured far greater hardship and cruelty than they had faced under the Tsars. Disastrous policies, such as the collectivization of agriculture (where small farms were grouped together under state control in one large 'collective'), caused famines in which millions died. Stalin gave orders for notorious 'purges', in which his real and imagined opponents were imprisoned or slaughtered indiscriminately in the name of communism. Huge numbers of people perished in slave labour camps or before firing squads. But, at the same time, Russia was transformed into a modern industrial nation. Factories, steel works, hydro-electric dams were built, all of which would help the Soviet Union compete with its hostile Western neighbours.

Stalin's policies brought terrible hardship to the people of the Soviet Union. Here, a Ukrainian woman poses with her starving infant during a famine in the 1930s.

Rapid industrialization under Stalin in the 1930s enabled the Soviets to resist the Nazi invasion of 1941.

Triumphant Soviet troops display captured Nazi regimental banners during a 1945 victory parade in Moscow.

IN 1941, DURING THE SECOND WORLD WAR, THE German army under the leadership of the Nazis invaded the Soviet Union. This act helped to turn the world's first communist state into a superpower. By 1945 Soviet armies had pushed the Germans back to Berlin. They then stayed there, and in the countries of Eastern Europe, for the next forty-five years. The hostility shown towards the Soviet Union by her Western neighbours inspired Stalin to set up a 'buffer zone' between the USSR and the West. Here, in Eastern European countries such as East Germany, Hungary and Czechoslovakia, any opposition to communism was ruthlessly suppressed. In the German city of Berlin, a wall was built between the Soviet-occupied east side and the areas held under Western control. This 'Berlin Wall' became a symbol of the inhumanity of the Soviet regime.

The Soviet Union's victory over the Nazis cost the country twenty million lives. But, after the war, Soviet citizens had the opportunity to enjoy the fruits of their victory and reap some benefit from the transformation of their nation during the 1920s and 1930s. New state-provided housing (row upon row of apartment blocks) brought a degree of comfort to those who had previously lived in terrible conditions. The state provided excellent health care, care for the elderly, and schools and universities, which produced new generations of well-educated men and women. In 1957, Soviet technology astonished the world when the USSR launched the world's first space satellite.

However, the Soviet Union carried the seeds of its own destruction. The terror people experienced under Stalin resulted in a country that was rigid, both with fear and in the way in which it conducted its affairs. After his death in 1953, Stalin was succeeded by Nikita Khrushchev. But when Khrushchev fell from power in 1964 there followed a line of usually dull, uncreative leaders. These were the 'years of stagnation' – a period marked by economic and social decay. The years from 1945 onwards were also the era of the 'Cold War' – a period of intense hostility and tension between the Soviet Union and the Western powers it had fought alongside during the Second World War. Both the Soviet Union and the West devoted vast resources to building up their armed forces. In particular they developed increasingly complex nuclear weapons which, if unleashed, could have destroyed human civilization. Although the Soviets and the Western powers never fought directly with one

Western leaders warmed to Mikhail Gorbachev. Here, he and US President Ronald Reagan sign a treaty concerning the control of nuclear weapons in 1987.

Perestroika and Glasnost

" More socialism means more democracy (and) openness... in everyday life. "

" The market is not an invention of capitalism. It has existed for centuries. It is an invention of civilization. "

" Jesus was the first socialist, the first to seek a better life for mankind. "

Mikhail Gorbachev, quoted above, attempted to bring democracy to the Soviet Union. With it, he brought about his own fall from power.

another, they each lent support and weapons to pro- or anti-communist forces in Korea, Cuba, Vietnam, Chile and other countries.

In 1986, the Chernobyl nuclear power plant in the Ukraine exploded. This accident, brought about by a lethal combination of poor training, robotic obedience to authority and a curiously Soviet lack of 'safety culture' (a common disregard for the lives of ordinary people) pointed to everything that was wrong with the society the Russian Revolution had produced.

In 1985 the great Soviet reformer Mikhail Gorbachev came to power, and introduced policies of *Perestroika* (restructuring) and *Glasnost* (openness) intending to improve his country's economic and political system and rescue it from the 'years of stagnation'. In the less repressive atmosphere ushered in by Gorbachev, the buffer states of Eastern Europe rebelled. They demanded, and won, their independence. The Communist Party mounted a coup in an attempt to cling on to its rapidly dwindling power. This failed but it forced Gorbachev's resignation. The Soviet Union became a democracy, with the election as president of Boris Yeltsin and his successor Vladimir Putin.

The Soviet Union is now known as the Commonwealth of Independent States. It is made up of Russia and eleven former countries of the Russian and Soviet empire, such as Ukraine, Belarus and Georgia, which are now independent nations. The Commonwealth is in a dangerous condition. Citizens have greater personal freedom, and access to Western goods. But corruption, poverty and crime are rife, and an older generation is left bitterly to reflect that the sacrifices they made for the communist state have ultimately been in vain.

Stalin's successor, Nikita Khrushchev, shares a joke with Mao Tse-tung, leader of communist China, in 1963.

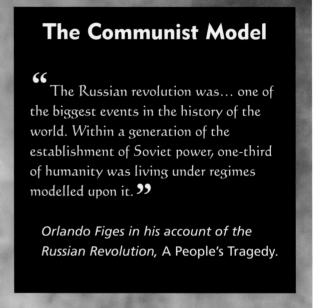

The Communist Model

"The Russian revolution was... one of the biggest events in the history of the world. Within a generation of the establishment of Soviet power, one-third of humanity was living under regimes modelled upon it."

Orlando Figes in his account of the Russian Revolution, A People's Tragedy.

IF LENIN HAD NOT PUSHED THROUGH THE RUSSIAN Revolution in those late October days of 1917, the history of the twentieth century would have been very different. Perhaps Russia would have evolved its own constitutional monarchy, along British lines, or become a democratic republic, like the United States. And, quite apart from the upheaval and tragedy that Russia's communist regime visited upon its own people, the effect that the Russian Revolution had on the rest of the world was enormous.

In Germany, fear of communism was one of the reasons for the rise of Adolf Hitler's Nazi Party. The German dictator's loathing and contempt for the Soviet Union led him to invade the country during the Second World War. This event ultimately led to the defeat of Germany and to the Soviet occupation of Eastern Europe for almost half a century.

After the Second World War, when the Soviet Union became a superpower, its wartime friendship with Britain and the United States turned to the open suspicion and hostility of the Cold War. With both sides possessing nuclear weapons of massive destructive power, the world seemed to stand on the brink of annihilation, especially during the Cuban Missile Crisis of 1962. The nuclear arms race, where each side competed with the other to develop more effective weapons and defences against them, consumed billions of dollars and roubles that could have been spent on constructive and beneficial enterprises.

The leaders of Russia's Revolution had hoped that other European nations would follow their example. This never happened, and the only communist regimes to emerge were those that had been imposed by the Russians in Eastern Europe after the Second World War. But nations elsewhere in the world followed the Soviet example. In the years after the Second World War, communist regimes came to power in China, Cuba, North Vietnam and North Korea.

From the excesses of Stalin's purges in the 1930s through to the continued use of labour camps and mental hospitals for 'dissidents' (opponents of the regime) in the 1980s, the cruelty of Russia's communist regime cannot be doubted. But not everything the Soviets did to Russia was for the worst. Today many Russians greatly miss the health care and social welfare system the communists provided.

A US aircraft flies low over a Soviet ship off the coast of Cuba during the Cuban Missile Crisis. American fears of Soviet nuclear missiles being set up in communist Cuba threatened to lead to a Third World War.

Perhaps the Russian Revolution's greatest legacy was that it saved the Soviet Union from Nazi occupation. When the Germans invaded in 1941, their aim was to conquer European Russia and reduce its people to slaves. Without the newly constructed steel works and factories of the 1930s, which turned out tanks, guns and aircraft in their thousands, and without Stalin's iron-handed leadership, it is possible that the Russian people may never have been able to withstand their inhuman Nazi opponents. By resisting with such courage and determination, the Soviets ensured that Hitler would fail in his ambition to dominate Europe. Without Soviet resistance, the forces of the United States and British Empire would have had to face Nazi Germany alone. Then, defeating a Nazi empire which stretched from the Atlantic to the Ural mountains and beyond, would have proved infinitely more costly, if not impossible.

Russia today: eighty years after the Revolution, Western-style capitalism is much in evidence.

Glossary

abdication When a ruling monarch voluntarily gives up his or her position.

absolute power Complete and unchallengeable power.

anti-Semite A person who is violently prejudiced against Jews.

atheists People who do not believe in any kind of god.

autocracy A form of government where supreme power rests with one person – in pre-revolutionary Russia's case power rested with the Tsar.

Bolsheviks In revolutionary Russia, a faction of the Social Democrats which followed Lenin.

cadet A trainee member of the armed forces.

charisma An indefinable personal quality which leads people to admire and follow the person possessing it.

Cold War An era of history following the Second World War, characterized by extreme suspicion and hostility between the Soviet Union and its allies and the United States and its allies.

conscription The compulsory calling up of men and women for the armed services.

constitution A set of rules by which a government operates.

constitutional monarchy A monarchy whose power is limited by a set of rules.

counter-revolution Opposition to a revolutionary government.

coup A sudden seizing of power, usually by military force.

courtiers People who are on close terms with a monarch and his or her family.

Cuban Missile Crisis An incident in 1962 when the United States tried to prevent Russian missiles from being sent to Cuba. Many people believe the crisis could have led to a nuclear war.

delegate A person chosen to represent a particular group or organization at a conference or meeting.

democracy A system of governing a country where the government is chosen by the people of that country.

democratic republic A democracy without a monarch.

dissidents A term used by the Soviet government to describe people inside the Soviet Union who opposed the regime.

dynasty A sequence of rulers from the same family.

fait accompli Something that has been done already and is pointless to discuss further.

famine Widespread starvation across a whole region.

fugitive Someone who is on the run from the police.

garrison Troops based at a fort.

governor-general In this case, the chief government representative in Moscow.

haemophilia An inherited disease characterized by an inability of blood to clot, and the constant danger of bleeding to death.

left-wing Broadly speaking, a political perspective which is socialist or communist.

legislature A group of people with the power to make or change laws.

liberals Political moderates who walk a middle way between the more extreme policies of left or right-wing political groups.

Marxist A supporter of Karl Marx, the political philosopher who inspired the communist policies of the Bolsheviks.

Mensheviks In revolutionary Russia, a faction of the Social Democrats who did not support Lenin.

military commissar An official in the Communist Party who has authority in the armed forces.

minister of munitions The government minister responsible for the manufacture and distribution of shells, ammunition and weapons.

mutiny Open rebellion against authority.

Nazis A political party elected in Germany in 1933 under the leadership of Adolf Hitler.

Orthodox Church Broadly speaking, the main version of Christianity in Russia.

pogrom A massacre of a racial or religious group.

premier The prime minister of a country.

Provisional Government A group of ministers ruling Russia after the abdication of the Tsar. They intended to hold democratic elections as soon as conditions allowed – hence the term 'provisional'.

rationing A means of distributing a limited supply of food to ensure that everyone gets a fair share.

reparations A sum of money paid by a conquered nation to a victorious nation, as compensation for losses incurred in a war.

right-wing Broadly speaking, a political perspective which is conservative, pro-monarchist, or fascist.

secret police A branch of state security concerned with political opponents of a regime, rather than criminals.

Slavs An ethnic group originating in Eastern Europe and European Russia.

social revolutionaries Opponents of the Tsar, whose strongest support came from the Russian peasantry.

social welfare system State support of citizens to ensure their basic needs are met.

ultimatum A particular demand which, if refused, is backed up with the threat of drastic action.

Western powers The United States and Canada and the democracies of Western Europe.

Further Information

Books for Younger Readers

The Russian Revolution by Tony Allan (Heinemann Library, 2002)

Lenin and the Russian Revolution by Steve Philips (Heinemann Educational, 2000)

The Russian Revolution by Adrian Gilbert (Wayland, 1995)

Books for Older Readers

A People's Tragedy by Orlando Figes (Pimlico, 1997)

The Russian Revolution by Anthony Wood (Longman, 1986)

Ten Days That Shook the World by John Reed (Penguin, 1977)

Dr Zhivago by Boris Pasternak (Collins, 1958)

Timeline

1894 Nicholas II succeeds his father Alexander III as Tsar. He also marries Alexandra of Hesse in this year.

1903 The Social Democratic Party splits into two rival factions – the Mensheviks and the Bolsheviks.

1904-5 Russia is defeated in the disastrous Russo-Japanese War.

January 1905 The 'Bloody Sunday' massacre begins a year of unrest, strikes and rebellion.

October 1905 The Tsar issues his 'October Manifesto' promising constitutional changes. Also in this year, Rasputin becomes a regular visitor to the royal household.

1906 The 'Fundamental Laws' confirm that the Tsar will not give up his autocratic power. The first Duma is called, but dissolved soon after.

1914 The First World War begins.

1915 Tsar Nicholas appoints himself commander-in-chief of the army.

1916 Rasputin is murdered.

February 1917 Tsar Nicholas is forced to abdicate as Russia descends into revolutionary chaos. Provisional Government set up.

October 1917 The Bolsheviks seize power in Petrograd (formerly St Petersburg).

March 1918 Trotsky presides over the Treaty of Brest-Litovsk, which ends the war with Germany and Austro-Hungary. Civil war breaks out between Bolshevik (Red) and pro-monarchist (White) forces.

July 1918 Nicholas II and his family are murdered at Ekaterinburg.

1920 Civil war ends with victory for the Red Army.

1921 Lenin introduces the New Economic Policy.

1924 Lenin dies and is eventually succeeded by Josef Stalin who, by 1927, is Russia's unchallenged leader.

1939 The Second World War begins.

1941 The Soviet Union is invaded by Nazi Germany.

1945 The Soviet Union defeats Germany, but remains in Eastern Europe as an occupying power.

1945-1989 An era known as the Cold War sees a period of great tension and hostility between the Soviet Union and Western Europe and the United States.

1954 Death of Stalin.

1985 Mikhail Gorbachev becomes leader of the USSR.

1989 The Cold War ends with gradual Soviet withdrawal from Eastern Europe.

1991 The USSR breaks up, and is replaced by the Commonwealth of Independent States.

In this poster from the early 1920s, Lenin strides confidently into a communist future.